# MY ÁNTONIA

*Willa Cather*

EDITORIAL DIRECTOR Justin Kestler
MANAGING EDITOR Ben Florman

SERIES EDITORS Boomie Aglietti, Justin Kestler
PRODUCTION Christian Lorentzen

WRITERS Jim Cocola, Brian Phillips
EDITORS Jane Carr, Benjamin Morgan

This edition published by Spark Publishing

Spark Publishing
A Division of SparkNotes LLC
120 Fifth Avenue, 8th Floor
New York, NY 10011

Any book purchased without a cover is stolen property, reported as "unsold and destroyed" to the Publisher, who receives no payment for such "stripped books."

02 03 04 05 SN 9 8 7 6 5 4 3 2 1

Please send all comments and questions or report errors to feedback@sparknotes.com.

Library of Congress information available upon request

Printed and bound in the United States

RRD-C

ISBN 1-58663-384-8

# Introduction:
## Stopping to Buy Sparknotes on a Snowy Evening

Whose words these are you *think* you know.
Your paper's due tomorrow, though;
We're glad to see you stopping here
To get some help before you go.

Lost your course? You'll find it here.
Face tests and essays without fear.
Between the words, good grades at stake:
Get great results throughout the year.

Once school bells caused your heart to quake
As teachers circled each mistake.
Use SparkNotes and no longer weep,
Ace every single test you take.

Yes, books are lovely, dark, and deep,
But only what you grasp you keep,
With hours to go before you sleep,
With hours to go before you sleep.

# CONTENTS

# CONTEXT

**W**ILLA CATHER WAS BORN on December 7, 1873, in rural Virginia. At the age of nine, she moved with her family to Red Cloud, Nebraska, where she spent the remainder of her childhood. After graduating from the University of Nebraska at Lincoln in 1895, she moved to Pittsburgh to begin a career in journalism. In all, Cather spent five years in the Pittsburgh newspaper and magazine trade, working at *Home Monthly* and the *Pittsburgh Leader*. Between 1901 and 1906 she taught high school English and Latin in Pittsburgh and the Pittsburgh area. During this period, she began to publish her first short stories. These early successes led to a position in New York City with *McClure's*, a magazine that often featured investigative journalism, where Cather served as an editor for six years.

In 1912 Cather published her first novel, *Alexander's Bridge,* which received a lukewarm reception. The next year, Cather caught the attention of the literary world with the appearance of *O Pioneers!*, exploring and celebrating frontier life in the American West. In 1918 she made her most lasting contribution to her status as one of the most celebrated post–Civil War American authors with the publication of *My Ántonia*. Like many of Cather's novels, *My Ántonia* fictionalizes recollections of her youth in rural Nebraska.

Though the narrative of *My Ántonia* is fictional, there are many similarities between Cather's life and that of the novel's protagonist. As Cather did, Jim Burden moves from Virginia to Nebraska as a child to live with grandparents; the town of Black Hawk, to which Jim and his grandparents move, is a fictionalized version of the Red Cloud of Cather's youth. Also as Cather did, Jim attends the University of Nebraska at Lincoln and eventually moves from Nebraska to New York.

If certain of the situations in the novel derive from Cather's recollections of her youth, however, the novel's high stature in American literature results from Cather's ability as a writer. Her sensitivity to the prairie landscape and her elegantly uncomplicated prose style have earned her a spot among America's finest novelists, and *My Ántonia* continues to stand as the most lasting hallmark of her skill. *My Ántonia* is generally considered a modernist novel. In the early twentieth century, many authors were concerned with the alienation from society that resulted from ongoing processes of mechanization and industrialization. These writers responded to what they perceived as an increased fragmentation of the world by creating narratives and stories that were themselves fragmented. Cather participates in this tradition both by creating a novel whose plot does not have a highly structured form and by idealizing a pre-industrial life far from the noise and speed of the city.

Cather was most prolific during the 1920s, when she published many of her finest works. After being awarded the Pulitzer Prize for *One of Ours* in 1922, she also enjoyed popular successes with *The Professor's House* in 1925, *My Mortal Enemy* in 1926, and *Death Comes for the Archbishop* in 1927. In her final two decades, Cather continued to write short stories and novels, albeit with less frequency and refinement. Nevertheless, she enjoyed an extraordinary amount of attention and critical esteem in her lifetime. In 1930 she won the Howells Medal for Fiction, and in 1944 she was awarded the gold medal of the National Institute of Arts and Letters.

Willa Cather died on April 24, 1947, in New York City, where she lived for thirty-nine years with her companion, Edith Lewis. Her reputation equalled that of any published American female novelist of her day, and critical and popular attention to her work continues to expand. Many critics place her firmly among such lauded American authors as William Faulkner and Ernest Hemingway, and there are those who would argue that hers is the single finest craft of her generation.

# Plot Overview

J IM BURDEN, A SUCCESSFUL NEW YORK CITY LAWYER, gives an acquaintance a memoir of his Nebraska childhood in the form of a recollection of their mutual friend, Ántonia Shimerda. This memoir makes up the bulk of the novel.

Jim first arrives in Nebraska at the age of ten, when he makes the trip west to live with his grandparents after finding himself an orphan in Virginia. On the train out west, Jim gets his first glimpse of the Shimerdas, a Bohemian immigrant family traveling in the same direction.

As fate would have it, the Shimerdas have taken up residence in farm neighboring the Burdens'. Jim makes fast friends with the Shimerda children, especially Ántonia, who is nearest to him in age and eager to learn English. Jim tutors Ántonia, and the two of them spend much of the autumn exploring their new landscape together.

In late January, tragedy strikes with the suicide of Mr. Shimerda. After an emotional funeral, the Shimerdas retreat into despair, and the Burdens struggle to be as accommodating as possible. As a result of the hardships that the Shimerdas suffer, Ántonia and Jim find that a wedge has been driven between them.

A couple of years later, the Burdens decide to move into town, and shortly thereafter Ántonia takes a job as a housekeeper with a neighboring family, the Harlings. Jim begins to see more of Ántonia once again, especially when a dancing pavilion comes to town and enlivens the social scene.

Jim's high school years quickly come to a close, and he is offered a spot at the university in Lincoln. He makes a great success of his high school commencement speech and spends the summer hard at work in preparation for his course of study. Before leaving, he takes one last trip out to the countryside with Ántonia and her friends, where they gather to reminisce about old times together.

In Lincoln, Jim throws himself into his studies, which take up the majority of his time in the first year and a half of his course. In the spring of his second year, he begins to see a good deal of Lena Lingard, a mutual friend of his and Ántonia's who has always intrigued Jim. After a few months of theatergoing and dalliances about town, Jim decides that he needs to make a fresh start of things and prepares to transfer to Harvard University for his final two years of college.

While Jim is away, Ántonia gets engaged to a local boy and moves to Denver in order to be with him. Days before the wedding, the boy abandons Ántonia, and she returns to Nebraska heartbroken. She covers up an unexpected pregnancy throughout its term, but in giving birth to a daughter incurs the disapproval of her family. However, she resolves to take care of her baby and continues to work on the farm with her brother.

After graduating from college, during the summer before entering law school, Jim returns to Nebraska to be with his grandparents. Upon hearing of Ántonia's situation, he decides to drive out to the countryside and visit her. They spend a happy day together reliving old times, and Jim parts with a promise to visit her again very soon.

Twenty years pass before Jim is able to visit Ántonia again. In the intervening period, he establishes himself as a prosperous New York City lawyer, and Ántonia marries and has many children with a man named Cuzak, also of Bohemian origin. Jim's visit to the Cuzak farm is a happy one, with plenty of laughter and stories. Ántonia and Jim renew their old ties, and Jim resolves to be in closer contact with the Cuzaks in the coming years.

As he prepares to leave Nebraska and return to New York City, Jim walks along the outskirts of town, near the overgrown road that leads to his childhood home. At peace with himself in this familiar landscape, he feels that his life has come full circle, and he reflects in the moonlight on all that his past with Ántonia has meant to him.

# CHARACTER LIST

*Jim Burden* The author of the youthful recollection that makes up the body of the novel. As a youth in Nebraska, Jim develops a close friendship with a Bohemian immigrant girl, Ántonia Shimerda. Jim is an intelligent, introspective young man who responds strongly to the land and the environment in which he lives. Unlike most other boys his age, Jim is more interested in academics and reflection than in roughhousing; in fact, he seems to prefer spending time alone or with girls such as Ántonia. At the time of the narrative's composition, Jim is married, but without children, and working as a legal counsel in New York City.

*Ántonia Shimerda* The focus of Jim's recollection, and one of his closest childhood friends. Ántonia moves to Nebraska from Bohemia with the rest of her family in her early teenage years. Intelligent, optimistic, loyal, and kindhearted, the naturally gregarious Ántonia is forced to accept a difficult life after the death of her father. At the time Jim writes the narrative, she is raising her large family on the Nebraska prairie, not far from where she and Jim grew up.

*Lena Lingard* A Norwegian immigrant's daughter and a friend of Ántonia's. Lena has a brief liaison with Jim in Black Hawk and a more extended relationship with him in Lincoln, where she sets up her own dressmaker's shop. Lena is pretty and blonde, and craves independence and excitement. Men are always attracted to her, but she refuses to marry and give up her freedom.

*Josiah Burden* Jim's grandfather. Josiah is a strongly religious man, silent and given to hard work.

*Emmaline Burden* Jim's grandmother. Emmaline shows great concern and compassion for the Shimerdas and is a loving maternal figure for Jim.

*Otto Fuchs* The Burdens' hired hand, who looks like a cowboy out of one of Jim's books but is actually an Austrian immigrant. Good-natured despite his rough appearance, Otto decides to seek his fortune in the West after the Burdens move to Black Hawk.

*Jake Marpole* Another hired hand of the Burdens. Jake makes the trip from Virginia to Nebraska along with Jim and accompanies Otto out west after the Burdens move to Black Hawk. Jake has a powerful temper but generally displays a good-natured and even childlike innocence about the world.

*Mr. Shimerda* The patriarch of the Bohemian immigrant family. A melancholy man given to artistic and scholarly pursuits, Mr. Shimerda feels very much out of place in foreign land. His depression eventually leads to suicide, leaving his family members to pick up the pieces and struggle to make a living on their own.

*Mrs. Shimerda* The matriarch of the Bohemian immigrant family. Mrs. Shimerda is a brusque, bossy, and often curt woman. After the suicide of her husband, she is forced to make do with the little that she has in an attempt to provide for her family.

*Yulka Shimerda* The youngest of the Shimerda children. Yulka is a pretty, young girl who later helps Ántonia raise her baby.

*Ambrosch Shimerda* The Shimerdas' oldest son. Mrs. Shimerda and her daughters dote on Ambrosch, claiming that he is brilliant and the reason they came to America. Ambrosch shares his mother's curt and presumptuous attitude, but becomes the unquestioned head of the family after Mr. Shimerda's suicide.

*Marek Shimerda* The younger of the two Shimerda brothers. Marek's physical deformities are accompanied by a handful of psychological instabilities and mental deficiencies.

*Tiny Soderball* One of the hired girls in Black Hawk and a friend to Ántonia and Lena. After working with Mrs. Gardener in the Boys' Home, Tiny travels west and makes a small fortune during the Alaskan gold rush.

*Russian Pavel* Tall, gaunt, and nervous, Pavel is an immigrant who falls ill under the care of the Shimerdas. He had been ostracized and forced to leave his native Russia after a frightful incident involving a wolf attack on a wedding party.

*Russian Peter* Pavel's housemate, and a fat, happy man. Like Pavel, Peter was forced into exile from his native Russia following a wolf attack on a wedding party. Peter eventually finds himself severely in debt and sells off his belongings, leaving America for a job as a cook in a Russian labor camp.

*Mr. Harling* The patriarch of the Harling family, neighbors to the Burdens in Black Hawk. A businessman of keen ability, Mr. Harling disapproves of Ántonia's frequent carousals at the dancing pavilion and eventually forces her to leave her post as their housekeeper because of her lifestyle.

**Mrs. Harling** The matriarch of the Harling family, and a charismatic and active woman. Mrs. Harling develops a strong affection for Ántonia, and she provides myriad activities for her children, Ántonia, and Jim, to take part in.

**Frances Harling** The oldest of the Harling children. Frances has a sound business mind and manages her father's accounts with a great deal of skill.

**Charley Harling** The only Harling son. Charley is of a military persuasion and eventually goes on to a successful career at the Naval Academy in Annapolis.

**Julia Harling** The middle Harling daughter. Julia is Jim's age and has a penchant for music.

**Sally Harling** The youngest Harling daughter, and something of a tomboy.

**Larry Donovan** Ántonia's fiancé, and an arrogant and selfish young man. After being fired from his job as a railroad conductor, Donovan leaves Ántonia on the eve of their wedding, running away to Mexico in search of a quick fortune.

**Mrs. Gardener** The proprietress of the Boys' Home in Black Hawk.

**Samson d'Arnault** A blind, black pianist. D'Arnault comes to Black Hawk on a blustery March weekend and gives a concert at the Boys' Home that brings down the house.

**Wick Cutter** The leading moneylender in Black Hawk and a shady character.

**Gaston Cleric** Jim's tutor at the university in Lincoln. Cleric eventually moves on to a teaching position at Harvard University and brings Jim along with him. His premature death from pneumonia has a strong effect on Jim.

*Widow Steavens* The Burdens' tenant at their old farmhouse. Widow Steavens develops a close relationship with Ántonia in the time surrounding the breaking of Ántonia's engagement.

*Anton Jelinek* A Bohemian homesteader and friend of the Shimerdas who later moves to Black Hawk and becomes a saloon proprietor.

*Peter Krajiek* A Bohemian immigrant and neighbor to the Burdens who sells the Shimerdas their first farm in America and cheats them out of several comforts.

*Cuzak* A Bohemian immigrant to America who marries Ántonia and raises a large family with her.

# ANALYSIS OF MAJOR CHARACTERS

## JIM BURDEN

Intelligent and introspective, Jim is well qualified to be the narrator of the story. His thoughtfulness gives him the ability to portray himself and others with consistency and sympathy and to convey the sense of a lost Nebraska with an evocative, poetic accuracy. Furthermore, his romantic nature and strong attachment to the people of his youth and to the Nebraska landscape give his narrative a sense of deep commitment and a longing, nostalgic quality that colors his story. The wistful nature of Jim's memoir highlights the novel's emphasis on the past as something personal to the individual who remembers it, which Jim acknowledges in choosing to call his memoir "*My* Ántonia" rather than "Ántonia." Jim is not claiming ownership of Ántonia; he is indicating that the story of Ántonia contained within his memoir is just as much a product of his own mind and heart as it is of the past.

Over the course of the novel, Jim ages from a ten-year-old boy into a middle-aged man, and grows from a shy orphan into a successful lawyer for the railroad companies, acquiring an impressive education along the way at the University of Nebraska and Harvard. In spite of the great changes that he undergoes, Jim remains a consistent character. He always has interest in others but is content to spend time alone; he often assumes the role of the detached observer watching situations unfold. The word "I" appears in *My Ántonia* with surprising infrequency, given the fact that the novel is a first-person memoir. Only at the end of the novel, when Jim sets aside his reservations to reunite with the middle-aged Ántonia on the Cuzak farm, does he seem to move past his passive role and make an active attempt to connect with the past he cannot forget.

Jim's most important relationship in the novel, of course, is his friendship with Ántonia, and the fact that he allows Ántonia to recede in his mind as an abstract symbol of the past is itself a strong illustration of Jim's introspective mentality. Rather than remaining close to Ántonia through the years, Jim allows himself to drift apart from her, always preserving her special place in his heart by treating her memory with greater and greater nostalgia as the years go by. Though the final segment of the novel—Jim's reunion with Ántonia after twenty years apart—is not presented as a staggering break-through, it nevertheless seems to be a great step forward in Jim's growth and maturity. He can at last contemplate re-creating a real relationship with Ántonia, acknowledging that she still exists and is still herself even after the past that they shared has ended.

## ÁNTONIA SHIMERDA

Captured by Jim in his nostalgic memoir of his younger days, Ánto-nia gradually emerges from Jim's emotional presentation of her to become a believable, independent character in her own right. In fact, by the end of the novel, Ántonia has perhaps made more of an impression on many readers than Jim has. Many critics argue that Ántonia, despite the fact that she barely appears in the last quarter of the novel, is the real protagonist. Pretty, vivacious, and extremely generous, Ántonia fascinates Jim. He feels that Ántonia is unusually alive, a sentiment that he echoes even after meeting her as the mother of ten children at the end of the novel.

Throughout the novel, Ántonia is caught between her natural optimism and cheer and the extremely difficult circumstances that she faces after her emigration from Bohemia and her father's suicide in America. She is also trapped by the cultural differences that make her feel like a perpetual outsider in Nebraska and lead, in part, to her inability to love Jim as more than a brother: the Shimerdas go hungry, and their poverty forces Ántonia to work as a servant girl; certain members of the Black Hawk community judge her harshly for her love of dancing; her fiancé betrays her and leaves her to raise a child alone. Yet she never loses her quality of inner grace and self-sufficiency. Ántonia always tries to make the best of her circum-stances, but she refuses to sacrifice her independence to improve her life. For example, she would rather work for the wretched Wick Cutter than follow Mr. Hartling's order to stop going to the dances.

Ántonia is based on an actual figure from Cather's childhood—a girl named Annie Pavelka, like Ántonia an immigrant and a hired girl in town whose father committed suicide. Cather admired Annie's inner radiance and her independence, and sought to capture those qualities in Ántonia. In the process, she created a character from whom the heart of her novel developed: Ántonia symbolizes the past, possesses a deep rapport with her landscape, and embodies the experiences of both immigrants and the Nebraska pioneers.

## LENA LINGARD

While Jim and Ántonia are by far the most important figures in *My Ántonia,* one should not overlook Lena's importance to Jim's youth (the third book of the novel bears her name as the title, indicating the extent of her impact on his life). Cather conjures Lena to contrast sharply with Ántonia: while Ántonia possesses an independence that gives her quiet inner strength, Lena craves excitement and autonomy, refusing to marry any of the men who fall in love with her beauty and charisma. Her choice to live in San Francisco is nearly as extreme for someone from Black Hawk as Jim's decision to move to New York.

It is no coincidence that Lena becomes important to Jim's life at the moment he begins to transition out of childhood and into adulthood. Just as Ántonia comes to embody Jim's memories of childhood innocence and purity, Lena, with her desire for sophistication and her precocious sexuality, comes to represent Jim's emergence as a young adult. Tellingly, Jim fantasizes sexually about Lena in a way that he cannot about Ántonia. Even as a young man in Black Hawk, Jim already associates Ántonia with a lost past and invests her with an aura of emotional purity that precludes sex. Lena continues to become more important to Jim as he attends college, when they are both in Lincoln together. Though Jim never grants Lena an exalted place in his memory as he does to Ántonia, she is still a pivotal figure in his growth from childhood to adulthood, and, given the importance he gives her in his story, she may continue to figure more largely in Jim's dream of the past than even Jim himself realizes.

# THEMES, MOTIFS & SYMBOLS

## THEMES

*Themes are the fundamental and often universal ideas explored in a literary work.*

### HUMANKIND'S RELATIONSHIP TO THE PAST

The central narrative of *My Ántonia* is a look into the past, and though in his narration Jim rarely says anything directly about the idea of the past, the overall tone of the novel is highly nostalgic. Jim's motive for writing his story is to try to reestablish some connection between his present as a high-powered New York lawyer and his vanished past on the Nebraska prairie; in re-creating that past, the novel represents both Jim's memories and his feelings about his memories. Additionally, within the narrative itself, characters often look back longingly toward a past that they have lost, especially after Book 1. Living in Black Hawk, Jim and Ántonia recall their days on the farms; Lena looks back toward her life with her family; the Shimerdas and the Russians reflect on their lives in their respective home countries before they immigrated to the United States.

The two principal qualities that the past seems to possess for most of the characters in the novel are that it is unrecoverable and that it is, in some way, preferable to the present. Ántonia misses life in Bohemia just as Jim misses life in Nebraska, but neither of them can ever go back. This impossibility of return accounts for the nostalgic, emotional tone of the story, which may have been autobiographical as well, informed by Cather's own longing for her Nebraska childhood. But if the past can never be recovered, it can never be escaped, either, and Jim is fated to go on thinking about Black Hawk long after he has left it.

The other important characteristic of the past in *My Ántonia* is that it is always personal: characters never look back toward bygone eras or large-scale historical conditions, but only toward the personal circumstances—places, people, things—that they remem-

000000

ber from their own lives. As a result, a character's emotions are destined to color his or her memories for the rest of his or her life, a fact that is made thematically explicit in the novel by Jim's decision to call his memoir "My Ántonia" rather than simply "Ántonia." In thus laying claim to Ántonia, Jim acknowledges that what he is really writing is simply a chronicle of his own thoughts and feelings.

The novel ends on an optimistic note, however, with Jim's return to Nebraska twenty years after he last saw Ántonia and his mature decision to visit more often and to keep Ántonia in his life. This decision implies that, by revisiting his past, Jim has learned to incorporate it into his present, to seek a real relationship with Ántonia rather than transform her into a symbol of the past in his own mind. The past, the novel seems to suggest, is unrecoverable, but the people who shared one's past can be recovered, even after a separation of many years.

## HUMANKIND'S RELATIONSHIP TO ITS ENVIRONMENT

Related to the novel's nostalgic feeling for the past is its in-depth exploration of humankind's relationship to its environment. What characters in *My Ántonia* miss about the past is not simply lost time but a lost *setting,* a vanished world of people, places, and things, especially natural surroundings. The characters in *My Ántonia* respond powerfully to their environments—especially Jim, who develops a strong attachment to the Nebraska landscape that never really leaves him, even after two decades in New York.

As Cather portrays it, one's environment comes to symbolize one's psychology, and may even shape one's emotional state by giving thoughts and feelings a physical form. The river, for example, makes Jim feel free, and he comes to prize freedom; the setting sun captures his introspective loneliness, and the wide-open melancholy of Nebraska's plains may play a role in forming his reflective, romantic personality—if it does not create Jim's personality, it at least comes to embody it physically. Thus, characters in *My Ántonia* often develop an extremely intense rapport with their surroundings, and it is the sense of loss engendered by moving beyond one's surroundings that occasions the novel's exploration of the meaning of the past.

## The Immigrant Experience in the United States

On a more concrete level, *My Ántonia* explores the lives of immigrants on the United States frontier in the second half of the nineteenth century. The Nebraska prairie of the novel is an ethnic hodgepodge combining American-born settlers with a wide range of European immigrants, especially eastern and northern Europeans such as the Bohemian Shimerdas, the Russians Peter and Pavel, and the Norwegian Lena. The novel creates a sympathetic portrait of the many hardships that immigrants faced, including intense homesickness (a form of longing for the past), inability to speak English, and a bewildering array of cultural and religious differences that the novel's immigrants must overcome if they wish to fit in with the often quite judgmental American settlers who make up the economic and cultural mainstream in Black Hawk. Because of the rigid (and, in Jim's eyes, preposterous) social hierarchy of Black Hawk, simply getting by can be very difficult for the immigrants, who lack the same opportunities as the Americans—Jim goes to school, for instance, while Ántonia must help her family eke out an existence after her father's suicide.

Still, though Cather's portrait of the immigrant experience is sympathetic, it never quite rises to the level of advocacy: Jim is describing a vanished past, not agitating for social change, and he himself shares many of the cultural assumptions of the American-born settlers. Thus, *My Ántonia* has little in common with more socially inflammatory works about the hardships faced by immigrants such as Upton Sinclair's *The Jungle,* which was written to bring about social change. *My Ántonia* is a much more personal story and is more concerned with re-creating an emotional reality than with awakening the nation to a moral outrage.

## The Traditional Nature of Frontier Values

*My Ántonia* evokes the living conditions and mindset of the nineteenth century, as well as the simple, hardworking, homespun ethic of that era's settlers, an ethic Cather approves of strongly even if she does not always approve of its application, for instance, the prejudicial treatment of the hired girls in town. The novel also explores the social assumptions of the frontier people on matters such as race (in the passage about Samson d'Arnault) and gender (in the passages about the hired girls, and in Jim's general desire to spend time with girls rather than with boys). These rigid traditional social assumptions require that Jim learn to fight and swear so that he will seem more like a boy. Nevertheless, despite their shortcomings, the settlers share values of family, community, and religion that make Black Hawk a close-knit and positive community, not unworthy of the nostalgia in which it is bathed throughout the novel.

## MOTIFS

*Motifs are recurring structures, contrasts, or literary devices that can help to develop and inform the text's major themes.*

### CHILDHOOD AND ADULTHOOD

As the generation to which the main characters (Ántonia, Jim, and Lena) belong grows from young children into adults, the novel indirectly evokes many of the characteristics and feelings of children as they make the transition into adulthood. As a result, the vanished past for which many of the characters long is often associated with an innocent, childlike state that contrasts with the more worldly, grown-up present. But the motif of childhood and adulthood is propagated in the novel mostly by the feelings of the characters as they gradually begin to experience independence, responsibility, and sexuality, leading to a natural contrast between the before and after states of their lives. Once Jim begins to fantasize sexually about Lena, his earlier years become less relevant; once Ántonia begins to live for the town dances, she is never again the same simple farm girl. In marking these sorts of divisions, the novel charts the growth of its principal characters, who eventually gain the maturity to understand the relationship between their past and their present.

### RELIGION

Of all the cultural differences between the European immigrants and the American settlers (and there are many, often complicated differences, as we see when Jim's grandmother attempts to give the Shimerdas a gift of food), the one that recurs most interestingly is the difference in religion. Most of the Europeans are Catholic, as the Shimerdas are, and most of the Americans are Protestant, as the Burdens are. In addition to this dichotomy, there are smaller cultural differences, such as language and attitude, which the novel explores from time to time. The motif of religion is most visible during the novel's depictions of Christmas and the circumstances surrounding Mr. Shimerda's suicide.

# SYMBOLS

*Symbols are objects, characters, figures, or colors used to represent abstract ideas or concepts.*

### THE NEBRASKA LANDSCAPE

The most important and universal symbol in *My Ántonia* is the Nebraska landscape. Cather's poetic and moving depiction of it is perhaps the most famous and highly praised aspect of the novel. The landscape symbolizes the larger idea of a human environment, a setting in which a person lives and moves. Jim's relationship with the Nebraska landscape is important on its own terms, but it also comes to symbolize a great deal about Jim's relationship with the people and culture of Nebraska, as well as with his inner self. Throughout the novel, the landscape mirrors Jim's feelings—it looks desolate when he is lonely, for instance—and also awakens feelings within him. Finally, the landscape becomes the novel's most tangible symbol of the vanished past, as Jim, the lawyer in distant New York, thinks back longingly on the landscape of his childhood.

### THE PLOW

The plow, which Jim and Ántonia see silhouetted against the enormous setting sun, symbolizes the connection between human culture and the natural landscape. As the sun sets behind the plow, the two elements are combined in a single image of perfect harmony, suggesting that man and nature also coexist harmoniously. But as the sun sinks lower on the horizon, the plow seems to grow smaller and smaller, ultimately reflecting the dominance of the landscape over those who inhabit it.

# SUMMARY & ANALYSIS

## INTRODUCTION–BOOK I, CHAPTER VI

*[T]his girl seemed to mean to us the country, the
conditions, the whole adventure of our childhood.*
(See QUOTATIONS, p. 49)

### SUMMARY: INTRODUCTION

The novel opens with an unnamed narrator recounting a train trip
through Iowa the previous summer with an old friend named Jim
Burden, with whom the narrator grew up in a small Nebraska town.
The narrator recalls talking with Jim about childhood on the prairie, and then notes that while they both live in New York, they don't
see each other much, since Jim is frequently away on business and
since the narrator doesn't really like Jim's wife. The narrator
resumes talking about the train trip with Jim through Iowa, adding
that their discussion kept returning to a girl named Ántonia, with
whom the narrator had lost touch but with whom Jim had renewed
his friendship. The narrator recounts that Jim mentioned writing
down his memories of Ántonia; the narrator expressed to Jim an
interest in reading these writings. A few months later in New York,
according to the narrator, Jim brought a portfolio of writings about
Ántonia to show to the narrator. The narrator adds that Jim, want-
ing to title the work, wrote "Ántonia" across the front of the portfolio before frowning and scribbling "My" before "Ántonia."

### SUMMARY: CHAPTER I

As the narrative begins, Jim is ten years old, newly orphaned and
making the trip west from Virginia to stay with his grandparents in
Black Hawk, Nebraska. He is traveling in the company of a farmhand named Jake Marpole, who is slightly older but who, like Jim,
has limited experience of the wider world. Beyond Chicago, a
friendly conductor informs Jim that an immigrant family, the
Shimerdas, are also bound for Black Hawk. Among this Bohemian
family, the only one who speaks any English is Ántonia, a young girl
about Jim's age.

Once the train reaches Black Hawk, Jim and Jake disembark, and one of the Burdens' hired men, Otto Fuchs, meets them. Before departing for the Burden farm, Jim observes the Shimerdas preparing to set off as well. The emptiness of the Nebraska landscape at night overwhelms Jim as he travels in the jolting wagon. Eventually, he falls asleep on a bed of straw as the wagon travels into the night.

### SUMMARY: CHAPTER II

The next afternoon, at the farm, Jim's grandmother, Mrs. Burden, awakens him and draws a bath for him. Afterward, Jim explores his new surroundings while Mrs. Burden prepares the evening meal. At supper, Jake discusses Virginia with the Burdens. Later, Otto tells stories of ponies and cattle to Jim, and the evening concludes with some family prayers. In the morning, Jim begins to take in the landscape around the farm. When he accompanies Mrs. Burden to the garden to pick potatoes for supper, he stays behind after her and sits quietly among the pumpkins.

### SUMMARY: CHAPTER III

On Sunday, the Burdens head out in the wagon to greet their new Bohemian neighbors. Mrs. Burden explains that someone took advantage of the Shimerdas when they decided to move to Black Hawk by overcharging for a farmhouse not suited to the harsh Nebraska winters. Mrs. Shimerda greets the Burdens upon arrival, and Mrs. Burden presents her with some loaves of bread. They exchange greetings, and, as the adults begin talking, Jim and Ántonia run off to play with her youngest sister, Yulka, trailing behind. As they wander through the grass, Jim teaches Ántonia a few English words. When the Burdens prepare to depart, Mr. Shimerda entreats Mrs. Burden to teach English to Ántonia.

### SUMMARY: CHAPTER IV

Later that same day, Jim takes his first of many long pony rides. As he rides, he reflects on Otto's story that the sunflowers that fill the prairies sprang from seeds scattered by Mormons on their way to Utah. Jim rides twice a week to the post office, and he describes many other rides that he takes simply to wander or explore the local wildlife, with Ántonia accompanying him at times. Jim begins giving Ántonia regular English lessons, and she loves to help Mrs. Burden around the house.

SUMMARY: CHAPTER V

One afternoon in late autumn, Ántonia takes Jim to visit a pair of Russian immigrants whom her family has befriended. Only Peter is at home, but he shows Ántonia and Jim his milking cow and feeds them a snack of melons. He then entertains them by playing a number of tunes on his harmonica. As Ántonia and Jim leave, Peter presents Ántonia with a sack of cucumbers for her mother, along with a pail of milk to cook them in.

SUMMARY: CHAPTER VI

On another fall day, near sunset, Ántonia and Jim encounter Mr. Shimerda, who has recently caught three rabbits. This bounty will provide food for the family and a winter hat for Ántonia. Mr. Shimerda promises to give his gun to Jim when Jim is older. Jim notes that Mr. Shimerda seems sad, which leaves a deep impression on Jim. As daylight wanes, the Shimerdas return to their farm, and Jim races his shadow home.

---

ANALYSIS: INTRODUCTION–BOOK I, CHAPTER VI

Several sections of *My Ántonia* preface the novel's actual narrative: in addition to the introduction, Cather includes an epigraph and a dedication. The epigraph, from Virgil's *Georgics* (a long poem about farming life), reads: "Optima dies . . . prima fugit," a Latin phrase meaning "The best days are the first to flee." Cather's dedication—"To Carrie and Irene Miner" above the words "In memory of affections old and true"—further emphasizes the nostalgic intent of the novel. From the very beginning, *My Ántonia* presents itself unmistakably as a novel imbued with strong yearnings for a vanished past.

Yet certain elements of the novel temper this nostalgic intensity. First and foremost, Cather provides a frame for the narrative by way of a narrated introduction, which gives the reader some psychological distance from the intensely personal voice of the memoir that forms the core of the novel. Although the introduction's content is fairly straightforward, it remains a curious document nonetheless— indeed, we are not sure whether we are supposed to consider the introduction as fact or fiction. The only concrete biographical information revealed about the narrator of the introduction concerns a childhood spent in rural Nebraska and a present existence in New York. While it may be plausible to assume that this narrator is

Cather herself, given that Cather has these locales in common with the narrator, the text offers no proof of this hypothesis.

Several critics have noted *My Ántonia* as a bold departure from American literature of its time, one of the first novels written by a woman to feature a male narrator and deserving of special attention because of the autobiographical elements in the text. Jim begins the novel as a ten-year-old orphan, moving cross-country from Virginia to Nebraska to live with his grandparents. Although Cather was not orphaned at age ten, she too made the move from Virginia to Nebraska to live with her grandparents, and the change of scenery had a profound effect upon her experience and her memory. It is always difficult to assess the importance of biography and invention in fiction, but it seems reasonable to assume that Cather employs a liberal amount of each. Cather was a rather tomboyish child, a trait that would certainly enhance her own capacity to get inside the head of a male narrator. In addition, her many intense childhood and adult friendships with women would allow her to paint a nostalgic picture of an immigrant frontier girl. To say that Cather herself is Jim Burden, however, may be to overstep the mark. Rather, it is Cather's willingness to combine biographical recollection with fictional experimentation (the use of a male narrator, for example) that merits note.

Jim's remark, upon presenting his portfolio to the narrator in the introduction—"I didn't take time to arrange it; I simply wrote down pretty much all that her name recalls to me. I suppose it hasn't any form"—prefigures the novel's extremely episodic nature. The memoir, the core of the novel, features little snippets of memory pasted loosely together. In place of a focused plot, Cather gives her attention to lengthy descriptions of the characters who populate the novel and, perhaps even more important, of the austere landscape that they inhabit.

The close relationship between humans and their environment is a major theme in *My Ántonia* and one of the ideas that Cather explored throughout her literary career. In *My Ántonia*, the focus is on landscape—the natural, physical settings in which the characters live and move. Among Cather's characters, Jim is especially sensitive to his environment, to the point that he invests human qualities in the landscape around him. Because of the scarcity of trees in the area, for instance, Jim remarks, "we used to feel anxious about them, and visit them as if they were persons." His ability to treat trees as people reflects his compassion for nature.

MY ÁNTONIA ✦ 25

At other times, aspects of the landscape come to represent emotions or ideas for Jim. Although Jim realizes that botanists have demonstrated the sunflower to be native to the Nebraska region, he prefers to believe Otto Fuchs's story that the Mormons scattered the seeds from which the local sunflowers grew on their flight westward. For Jim, this romantic legend supersedes scientific explanation, and he prefers keeps the landscape as something to dream about, not necessarily as something to understand rationally.

## BOOK I, CHAPTERS VII–XIII

> *"I never know you was so brave, Jim," she went on comfortingly. "You is just like big mans. . . ."*
> (See QUOTATIONS, p. 50)

### SUMMARY: CHAPTER VII

One day, Ántonia and Jim ride Jim's pony to Peter's house to borrow a spade for Ambrosch, her older brother. On the way home, they stop to examine a group of prairie-dog holes. Suddenly, Ántonia spots an enormous snake and lets out a scream, which causes the snake to coil in their direction. She points at the snake and shouts at Jim in her native Bohemian. Jim turns around and sees the huge snake. He swiftly gathers his wits and uses the spade to bludgeon the snake several times to kill it. Jim gets angry at Ántonia for not warning him in English about the presence of the snake, but her admiration for his bravery quickly wins him over. They resolve to bring the dead snake home to show off Jim's victory. The size of the snake impresses Jim's elders, and Ántonia derives great pleasure from relating the story to all interested listeners.

### SUMMARY: CHAPTER VIII

Meanwhile, the Russians, Peter and Pavel, have fallen upon hard times. Peter finds himself deeply in debt to a Black Hawk money-lender named Wick Cutter, and Pavel seriously injures himself in a fall. When Peter arrives at the Burdens' to ask the Shimerdas, who are visiting, for help, Jim decides to accompany Ántonia and her father to the Russians' farm. They arrive after nightfall and find Pavel lying incapacitated. Frantic preoccupation with wolves punctuates his illness—a fascination whose origins Ántonia explains to Jim on the ride home: when Pavel and Peter were living in Russia, they attended a winter wedding party between a mutual friend and a girl from a neighboring town. On the ride home from the wedding, a pack of wolves attacked the wedding party in their sledges. Everyone perished, with the exception of Pavel and Peter, who were driving the sledge that carried the newly married couple; in a frantic effort to lighten that sledge's load to increase its speed, Pavel had thrown the couple to the wolves. The shame of this incident drove Pavel and Peter from their hometown and later from Russia.

The memory of the horror of that evening plagues both Pavel and Peter. Pavel dies mere days after Ántonia and Jim's visit, and, with Pavel gone, Peter sells off everything and leaves America. Mr. Shimerda thus quickly loses two of the only friends he had made in the country, and Pavel's story continues to fascinate Ántonia and Jim long after Pavel's death.

### SUMMARY: CHAPTER IX

At the first snowfall, Otto Fuchs builds a sleigh for Jim to drive. After a test run, Jim sets out to give Ántonia and Yulka a ride. The girls are unprepared for the cold weather, and Jim gives them some of his clothing to help them keep warm. As a result, he himself is vulnerable to the cold, and ends up bedridden for two weeks with quinsy, a severe tonsil disease.

### SUMMARY: CHAPTER X

Jim's next encounter with Ántonia occurs when Mrs. Burden resolves to bring a gift of a rooster and foodstuffs to the Shimerdas. As they approach the Shimerda farm, Jim spots Ántonia working at the water pump, but she quickly flees back to the house. When Mrs. Shimerda answers the Burdens' call, she is in tears. The Shimerdas have very little food stored up for the winter, and much of what they do have is rotting. When Jake brings in the gift basket of food, Mrs. Shimerda only cries harder. Mr. Shimerda explains that they were not beggars in Bohemia, but that several unexpected turns in America have left them with very little money. While Mrs. Burden reassures the Shimerdas, Jim plays with Yulka's kitten. As the Burdens rise to leave, Mrs. Shimerda presents a small gift package of food to Mrs. Burden. On the ride home, Jake and Mrs. Burden discuss the Shimerdas' plight. Later, while preparing supper, Mrs. Burden discards the gift package of food. Though he is unsure of what the food is, Jim breaks off a small piece and eats it anyway.

## SUMMARY: CHAPTER XI

During the week before Christmas, with Jake preparing to go into town to do the Burdens' Christmas shopping, a heavy snow begins to fall. Mr. Burden decides that the roads are unfit for travel, and the family sets about to create homemade Christmas presents. Jim makes a pair of picture books for Ántonia and Yulka, and Mrs. Burden bakes gingerbread cookies. After delivering an offering to the Shimerdas, Jake brings back a small cedar tree, which the Burdens decorate on Christmas Eve.

## SUMMARY: CHAPTER XII

On Christmas morning, Mr. Burden leads the family in prayer, and afterward they sit down to a meal of waffles and sausage. Jake mentions that the Shimerdas were very happy to receive gifts from the Burdens. In the afternoon, Mr. Shimerda arrives to thank the Burdens for all of their kindnesses. They persuade him to stay for supper, and he stays until well after dark.

## SUMMARY: CHAPTER XIII

By New Year's Day, a thaw has reduced the snow to slush. Soon after, when Mrs. Shimerda and Ántonia visit the Burdens, Ántonia and Jim have a fierce argument about the Shimerdas' situation and attitude. The mild weather continues until late January, when, on Jim's eleventh birthday, a violent snowstorm blankets the countryside and brings work on the farm to a grinding halt.

---

## ANALYSIS: BOOK I, CHAPTERS VII–XIII

*My Ántonia* proposes much bolder theories about gender than most other novels of its time. Not only does Cather, a female author, write in the first-person voice of a male narrator, Jim, but Jim himself chooses to spend very little time with the Shimerda boys. Instead, he focuses his attention almost exclusively on Ántonia and Yulka. Even in the face of a language barrier, a young frontier boy would be more likely to spend more time with his male peers than with his female peers. But Jim's sensitive nature and Ántonia's tomboyish eagerness for adventure make the two natural companions. If the characters of a novel can be thought of as aspects of their creator's persona, Ántonia and Jim are certainly complementary components of Cather. While growing up, Cather did not fit within traditional gender boundaries; she cut her hair short and called herself William.

Throughout her life, furthermore, she shunned heterosexual relationships and socially accepted gender norms. Likewise, the relationship between Ántonia and Jim breaks—or rather, ignores—the conventions of gender relations.

Jim reveals an especially strong desire to identify with his fellow human beings across all kinds of boundaries and differences. This urge to connect is tied closely to Jim's mystical belief that a divine presence is controlling his fate. As he rides in the back of a horse-drawn wagon, staring up at the stars, he speaks on behalf of Ántonia when he asserts that "though we had come from such different parts of the world, in both of us there was some dusky superstition that those shining groups have their influence on what is and what is not to be." Although Jim feels increasingly alienated from the world, he is comforted by the discovery that Ántonia, despite coming from a culture entirely different from his own, shares his belief about the stars and fate.

Although Jim is not as displaced as the Bohemians or the Russians, he too is an immigrant of sorts, and his desire to identify with others leads him to adapt the immigrant experience to his own life. After he hears Pavel's story of the wolves, for instance, Jim repeatedly imagines himself as a sledge driver in flight, "dashing through a country that looked something like Nebraska and something like Virginia." When he makes homemade picture books for Ántonia and Yulka at Christmas, he uses resources that he brought from Virginia, which he refers to as "my 'old country.' "

This desire for shared experience also manifests itself in Jim's efforts to bring the legends and stories of the Bible closer to his own experience. As Mr. Burden reads from the Book of Matthew on Christmas morning, the story of Jesus' birth strikes Jim as seeming like "something that had happened lately, and near at hand."

Mr. Shimerda's visit to the Burdens on Christmas Day puts a slight ripple in the harmony that Jim feels. Jim's sense of universality cannot override the practical gap in observance existing between different religions. While the Shimerdas are from Bohemia (a western region of the Czech Republic, a country with a substantial Catholic population) and of Catholic heritage, the Burdens are Protestant. Mr. Shimerda emphasizes this difference by kneeling in front of the Burdens' Christmas tree, transforming it from a symbolic decoration into an explicitly religious icon. While the Burdens may not identify, or even agree, with this type of religious observance, Mr. Burden decides to tolerate it quietly. "The prayers of all

SUMMARY & ANALYSIS

good people are good," he remarks as Mr. Shimerda vanishes into the Christmas night. It is a noble sentiment, but Cather is ambiguous about whether Mr. Burden speaks sincerely.

Jim himself reveals an uncharacteristic lack of sympathy in the argument he has with Ántonia shortly after New Year's Day, which may be attributed to his immaturity as a ten-year-old boy. While he retells the story in an adult voice, his words and actions in the story are those of his ten-year-old self. His inability to appreciate the complexity of the Shimerdas' situation in a new country is not a matter of insensitivity to their plight or scorn of foreigners, but rather a lack of adult perspective. While he tells Ántonia that "people who don't like this country ought to stay at home," it is clear from the attention and energy he pours into his relationship with Ántonia that her departure from Nebraska is the last thing he would want.

Ántonia and Jim's argument, as an unexpected turn in an otherwise pleasant narrative, suggests greater tensions to come. Additionally, Cather employs a change in the weather to foreshadow trouble. An unusually mild beginning to the year gives way to a violent blizzard. At this point, Cather uses an elegant metaphor of snowbound animals to represent the struggling immigrant family. The high drifts leave the guinea hens "resentful of their captivity," leading them to screech and attempt to poke their way out of the snow walls that have been built up around them. The Shimerdas, in their economic hardship, face a similar challenge in the unfamiliar land that they now inhabit.

## BOOK I, CHAPTERS XIV–XIX

*If I live here, like you, that is different. Things will be easy for you. But they will be hard for us.*

(See QUOTATIONS, p. 51)

### SUMMARY: CHAPTER XIV

On the second morning of the blizzard, Jim wakes to a great commotion. When he arrives in the kitchen, his grandfather informs him that Mr. Shimerda is dead. With Ambrosch Shimerda curled up on a nearby bench, the Burdens quietly discuss the apparent suicide as they eat breakfast. Jake describes Krajiek's strange behavior around the body and notes that Krajiek's axe fits the gash in Mr. Shimerda's face. Otto Fuchs and Mrs. Burden talk him out of his suspicions. After the meal, Otto sets out to summon the priest and the coroner from Black Hawk, and the others clear the road for the trip to the Shimerdas. Jim stays behind and finds himself alone. After completing a few chores, he settles down to contemplate Mr. Shimerda's death. At dusk, the wagon returns, and Jake describes the scene at the Shimerdas' to Jim.

## SUMMARY: CHAPTER XV

The next day, Otto returns from Black Hawk with a young Bohemian named Anton Jelinek. At dinner, Jelinek bemoans the fact that no priest could be found to put Mr. Shimerda to rest. Afterward, Jelinek goes out to clear a road to the Shimerdas' wide enough for a wagon, and Otto begins to construct a coffin. Later in the afternoon, a number of other locals stop at the Burdens' to ask after the Shimerdas and discuss the tragedy. The coroner refrains from issuing a warrant for Krajiek at Mr. Burden's urging. The postmaster alerts the Burdens that none of the graveyards in the area will accept Mr. Shimerda because he killed himself, and Mrs. Burden lashes out in bitterness at this unfairness. With no graveyard to turn to, the Shimerdas decide that they will bury Mr. Shimerda on the corner of their homestead.

## SUMMARY: CHAPTER XVI

After lying dead in the barn for four days, Mr. Shimerda is finally buried on his own land. Despite the beginnings of another ominous snowfall, rural neighbors come from miles around to attend the burial. At Mrs. Shimerda's request, Mr. Burden says a prayer in English for Mr. Shimerda, and afterward Otto leads the assembled group in a hymn.

## SUMMARY: CHAPTER XVII

With the coming of spring, the neighbors help the Shimerdas to build a new log house on their property, and they eventually acquire a new windmill and some livestock. One day, after giving an English lesson to Yulka, Jim asks Ántonia if she would like to attend the upcoming term at the schoolhouse. Ántonia proudly refuses, saying that she is kept too busy by farm work, but her tears of sorrow reveal her true feelings on the matter. Jim stays at the Shimerdas' for supper, but he is offended by their ingratitude over neighborly charity and by Ántonia's coarse manners.

## SUMMARY: CHAPTER XVIII

Once school starts, Jim sees less and less of Ántonia, and soon tension erupts between them. When Jake and Jim ride over to the Shimerdas' to collect a loaned horse collar, Ambrosch first denies borrowing it, then returns with a badly damaged collar he rudely gives over to them. After a heated exchange, Jake grabs Ambrosch, who kicks him in the stomach. Jake then pounds Ambrosch on the head. Jake and Jim quickly pull away from the Shimerdas', as Mrs. Shimerda yells after them about sending for the authorities.

When Mr. Burden learns of the incident, he sends Jake into town with a ten-dollar bill to pay the assault fine. For the next few weeks, the Shimerdas are proud and aloof when meeting the Burdens in passing, although they maintain their respect for Mr. Burden. Finally Mr. Burden arranges a reconciliation by hiring Ambrosch to help with his wheat threshing and offering Ántonia a job to help Mrs. Burden in the kitchen. In addition, he forgives Mrs. Shimerda her debt on the milk cow she bought from him. In an effort to show her own forgiveness, Mrs. Shimerda knits Jake a pair of socks.

## SUMMARY: CHAPTER XIX

In high summer, Ántonia and Jim spend more time together, walking to the garden each morning to collect vegetables for dinner. One night, during an electric storm in a light rain, Ántonia and Jim climb onto the roof of the chicken house to stare at the sky until they are called down for supper. Ántonia tells Jim that things will be easy for him but hard for her family.

## ANALYSIS: BOOK I, CHAPTERS XIV–XIX

Throughout the novel, Jim shows an extraordinary capacity to identify with others, and, upon hearing of Mr. Shimerda's apparent suicide, he immediately senses that "it was homesickness that had killed Mr. Shimerda." As Jim imagines the homeward route of Mr. Shimerda's released spirit through Chicago and Virginia, two way stations on his own journey to Nebraska, he identifies with the sense of loss that he believes caused Mr. Shimerda such disenchantment. In meditating on Mr. Shimerda's life, Jim comes to feel as though his memories almost "might have been Mr. Shimerda's memories."

Jim's most concentrated struggle with cultural difference occurs over the matter of religion. As Jake describes Ambrosch's view that his father has been sent to purgatory as a result of his suicide, Jim rails against what is to him an incomprehensible stance, saying, "I almost know it isn't true." But the "almost" indicates Jim's hesitation. Because he himself holds a belief that is mystical (his belief in the presence of Mr. Shimerda's soul), Jim is unable to rule out the seemingly unsupportable beliefs of others. As he attempts to sleep that night, Jim is crushingly preoccupied with this unfamiliar idea of purgatory, suggesting that his confrontation with other ways of thinking has left him uncomfortable. Although Jim listens carefully to Anton Jelinek's story of religious conviction and finds it "impossible not to admire his frank, manly faith," there is clearly a divide between the Bohemians' more instinctual faith and Jim's more philosophical spirituality.

The Nebraska prairie, as an amalgam of various immigrant groups, is a testing ground for collisions between such differing religious viewpoints. Mr. Shimerda's suicide proves to be a test case for the solidarity of the farming community. When the old-guard religions universally refuse to have a suicide buried in their graveyards, the Shimerdas are forced to come up with an alternative. In dismissing the conservative standards of the foreign churches, Mrs. Burden proposes "an American graveyard that will be more liberal minded." This American graveyard is a burial plot on the family land, accompanied by a makeshift funeral and an improvised service conducted by the farming community. For all of its unorthodoxy, the beauty of this service captures Jim's imagination, as he remarks on his affection for "the dim superstition" of the event and the "propitiatory intent" of the grave that remains behind it.

With Mr. Shimerda departed, the different paths that await Ántonia and Jim begin to emerge. Structurally, this chapter concludes Book I, the main phase of Jim and Ántonia's relationship in the rural countryside. The directions that they will take in life are already becoming visible, and they begin to grow apart. Thrown into a more laborious role on the farm, Ántonia quickly loses her feminine softness, and Jim's entry into school sets him off on an altogether separate road. Interestingly, in spite of, or perhaps because of, his more formal education, Jim fails to recognize the reality of this difference. When he says to Ántonia that he wishes she could always be "nice" rather than rough and tumble, she explains that "things will be easy for you. But they will be hard for us." Here, for the first time, Cather clearly presents the dichotomy between Ántonia's role as a rural worker and Jim's role as a leisured thinker—a dichotomy that she explores throughout the remainder of the novel.

# BOOK II, CHAPTERS I–VII

## SUMMARY: CHAPTER I

Almost three years after his move to Black Hawk, Jim and his grandparents decide to leave their farm in the countryside for a house on the outskirts of town. Finding himself out of work, Otto decides to head out west in search of adventure, and Jake decides to go with him. Before leaving, they help the Burdens move their household. One Sunday morning, they set off on a train, never to see Jim again.

Mr. Burden takes a post as a deacon at the Baptist church in Black Hawk, and Mrs. Burden helps out with the church's social calendar. Jim begins attending the school in town and quickly adjusts to the company of his new classmates. Jim questions Ambrosch for any news about Ántonia whenever Ambrosch comes to town, but Ambrosch is taciturn and says little.

## SUMMARY: CHAPTER II

The Burdens' nearest neighbors are the Harlings, a Norwegian family who also used to live on a farm. Three of the Harlings' children are around Jim's age, and their older sister, Frances, works in Mr. Harling's office. In August, the Harlings' cook leaves them, and Mrs. Burden convinces them to hire Ántonia.

## SUMMARY: CHAPTER III

With her warm personality and easy way, Ántonia is right at home among the Harlings, and she soon settles into a regular routine.

## SUMMARY: CHAPTER IV

One evening, a visitor calls for Ántonia at the Harlings'. Lena Lingard, a local farm girl, has come to announce that she has also found work in town, as a dressmaker. The Harlings welcome Lena, but Ántonia treats her coolly, unsure how she is meant to receive her visitor. Jim, thinking back to the stories he has heard of Lena, relates her entanglement with a neighboring farmer, Ole Benson, who became so smitten with Lena that his jealous wife attacked her.

## SUMMARY: CHAPTER V

During the autumn, Jim sees Lena often in town. He helps her to shop for fabric and they trade gossip and stories about life in Black Hawk. Shortly before Christmas, Jim sees Lena and her brother shopping for Christmas presents for their mother. Lena advises her brother to get her monogrammed handkerchiefs, and then, teary-eyed, tells Jim that she misses her family very much.

## SUMMARY: CHAPTER VI

As winter descends, Jim turns to various indoor amusements, playing at charades and dress-up and dancing with Ántonia and the Harlings in the evenings. Ántonia tells the Harlings a story about a man who, for no apparent reason, dove into a threshing machine and killed himself. The story upsets Nina Harling, but the memories of threshing time make Mrs. Harling homesick for the country.

## SUMMARY: CHAPTER VII

In March, with snow still covering the landscape, excitement fills Black Hawk when Samson d'Arnault, a blind, black pianist, comes to town. Jim makes his way to the Boys' Home, where d'Arnault and his manager are staying. He enters the parlor to find a raucous scene, a full house listening to music and gossiping away. Eventually, d'Arnault plays a concert of old plantation standards to an enthusiastic audience. During one of his numbers, d'Arnault senses the patter of women dancing in a neighboring room. A door opens to reveal Ántonia, Lena, and two of their friends dancing among themselves. After a bit of hesitation and plenty of encouragement from the men, the girls come into the parlor and join the party, dancing until d'Arnault's manager shuts the piano. After the party breaks up, Jim and Ántonia walk home together, excited and restless.

---

## ANALYSIS: BOOK II, CHAPTERS I–VII

Once Cather settles the Burdens comfortably in Black Hawk, her focused treatment of the landscape gives way to a scrutiny of the townspeople. She introduces several new characters in a very short time span, and, in turn, Jim's narrative becomes less purposefully sequential and more episodic and anecdotal. Whereas Cather earlier presents an idyllic portrait of a group of people overwhelmed by a place, the shift to Black Hawk is mirrored by a reduction of emphasis on the power and importance of the land and an increased emphasis on the individuals in the town. In a world of finance and industry, people have a more businesslike and economic relationship to each other, as epitomized by Frances Harling's utilitarian approach to her townspeople.

Another major contrast between the farm and the town is the emphasis that each environment places on gender roles. In the countryside, Jim is free to be domestic and sensitive in the company of women. But Jim's arrival in town forces him to recognize his social identity as a male. In adjusting to school and his classmates, he seems to become "quite another boy," learning to fight, swear, and tease the girls. The pressure to assume gendered behavior is equally acute on Ántonia, who gradually begins to make the shift from tomboyish farmhand to polished town girl. Lena Lingard also changes her costume, trading in her tattered farm rags for the smarter costumes of a dressmaker. Cather's title for Book II is "The Hired Girls," which serves as a reminder of the important connection among occupation, place, and sexuality, for both the young women and young men. This new pressure denotes another shift in the main characters' lives: just as Book I describes life in the country and Book II describes life in town, Book I describes the characters as children, while Book II describes them as young adults. The move to town comes with a new shift to more urban, grown-up interests, such as the dancing that takes place in Chapter VII.

Because the farm is associated with the past and the town with the present, Jim and Ántonia become nostalgic for their former existence in the country. Even Lena, who is most keen on the lures of the town life, confesses her nostalgia for her rural family life. While telling Jim one of her wild tales of adventure, she admits to him of her rustic family, "I get awful homesick for them, all the same."

Although the shift from farm to town marginalizes the landscape, the harsh climate of the Nebraska prairie continues to dominate the flow of the narrative. Jim finds the winter a nearly unendurable penalty for the pleasantness of summer. When Ántonia relates the story of a tramp who committed suicide by leaping into a thresher, the mystery for the Harlings is not in the tramp's choice to kill himself but that he did so in such a lovely season as late summer. It is as if the Harlings conceive of pleasant weather as a boon from their often unforgiving environment not to be taken for granted.

One of the few breaks in the monotony of Jim's first long winter in town is the visit paid to Black Hawk by Samson d'Arnault, the itinerant black pianist. While some may take offense at the coarse picture Cather paints of d'Arnault, it is difficult to imagine that the insensitive nature of her characterization was intentionally meant to wound. Although her descriptions of him at his piano—"enjoying himself as only a Negro can" and later, playing with a gusto "full of strong, savage blood"—may have been aimed to charm the audiences of 1918, they are more likely to provoke outrage in a modern reader. Nevertheless, her nostalgic and accurate portrait of part of America's past is of great value as a cultural document.

# BOOK II, CHAPTERS VIII–XV

> [The plow] stood out against the sun . . . the handles,
> the tongue, the share—black against the molten red.
> There it was, heroic in size, a picture writing on
> the sun.
> (See QUOTATIONS, p. 52)

### SUMMARY: CHAPTER VIII
Finally, the long winter gives way to spring, and Ántonia, Jim, and the Harling children spend their days in the garden and at play among the trees. In June, the Vannis, an Italian family, arrive with a dancing pavilion and begin giving lessons. The pavilion quickly becomes a center of town life, especially on Saturday nights, when the dancing carries on until midnight.

### SUMMARY: CHAPTER IX
Jim claims that all the socially respectable boys are secretly attracted to the country girls who came to Black Hawk as hired girls. But because of the town's extremely rigid social hierarchy, none of the town boys feels comfortable dating a hired girl. For his part, Jim finds the hired girls more interesting and worthwhile than the townsfolk, and he begins to spend time with them, to the general disapproval of the community.

### SUMMARY: CHAPTER X
Over time, Ántonia begins to draw notice at the pavilion, and thoughts of dancing soon preoccupy her waking hours. Trouble arises when an engaged boy attempts to kiss Ántonia on the Harlings' back porch. Although Ántonia manages to fight him off, Mr. Harling presents her with an ultimatum: she must quit dancing or look for work elsewhere. Indignant, Ántonia decides to take her chances on her own and announces her plan to find work with Wick Cutter, the local moneylender. Distraught, Mrs. Harling tells Ántonia that she cannot speak to her if she works for the Cutters. Ántonia insists on keeping her independence and leaving the Harlings.

## SUMMARY: CHAPTER XI

Jim describes the Cutters as a detestable Black Hawk couple, generally loathed by the populace: Wick Cutter is a devious moneylender who makes his money by manipulating farmers into accepting unwise loans, and Mrs. Cutter is a hideous shrew. The Cutters do not even get along with each other, and their epic arguments are legendary throughout the town.

## SUMMARY: CHAPTER XII

Once set up at the Cutters, Ántonia spends even more time and energy on her new social life. She sews her own outfits and parades around town with Lena and a number of the other hired girls. Now a senior in high school, Jim sometimes travels about with them. After the Vannis leave town, a group called the Owl Club begins to stage dances in the Masonic Hall each Tuesday, but Jim refuses to join. Envious of the older girls, Jim begins to grow restless at the thought of being cooped up in school, and so he visits a local saloon. When Jim's reputation is brought into question, he is forced to look elsewhere for diversion, but he quickly finds that very few diversions are to be found in Black Hawk.

Eager to find an alternative, Jim resolves to attend the Saturday night dances at the Firemen's Hall, sneaking out of the house after his grandparents have fallen asleep. One evening, after a night of dancing, Jim walks Ántonia back to the Cutters. When he asks for a kiss and goes a little farther than Ántonia expects, she scolds him for his brazenness. Jim, pleased at her show of virtue, walks home with his heart full of her.

## SUMMARY: CHAPTER XIII

A short time later, Jim notices that his grandmother has been crying. She has learned of his secret journeys to the Firemen's Hall dances, and she is ashamed of his deceitfulness. In an attempt to atone for his actions, Jim swears off the dances, but he finds himself lonely again as a result.

At his high school commencement, Jim gives an oration that the crowd receives wonderfully. Afterward, Ántonia breathlessly congratulates him and is moved to tears when he declares that he dedicated the oration to her father. Jim is thrilled with his success.

SUMMARY & ANALYSIS

## SUMMARY: CHAPTER XIV

During the summer, Jim commits himself to a rigorous study schedule in preparation for his upcoming university studies. His one holiday comes in July, when he arranges to meet a party of girls, including Ántonia and Lena, at the river. As he approaches, he spots Ántonia sitting alone by a stream and notices she has been crying. When Jim asks her why she is sad, she confesses to him her pangs of homesickness for the old country and for her father. Later in the day, Ántonia and Jim rejoin the rest of the girls, and they spend the afternoon playing games and talking together until sunset.

## SUMMARY: CHAPTER XV

Left alone to housesit for the Cutters in late August, Ántonia has an uneasy feeling about spending the night by herself. Jim agrees to sleep there in her stead and comes back to the Burdens each morning for breakfast. On his third night in the house, he is roused by a noise, but quickly falls back asleep. A short while later, he wakes to the noise of someone in the same room and comes face to face with Cutter, who was expecting to find Ántonia in the room. Cutter has used the trip as an elaborate scheme to abandon his wife and either seduce or rape Ántonia. He had told Ántonia that he left his valuables under her bed and that she must not leave them unattended at night. A scuffle ensues, and Jim manages to escape Cutter by leaping out of the window and running through the dark town in his nightshirt. He eventually makes his way home, only to find that he has suffered several severe bruises and cuts.

Jim holes up in his room to recover, and Mrs. Burden accompanies Ántonia to the Cutters to pack her trunk. They find the house in utter disarray, and, as they are gathering up the torn garments, Mrs. Cutter arrives at the front door. After doing her best to calm Mrs. Cutter down, Mrs. Burden listens in amazement as Mrs. Cutter relates the elaborate ruse that her husband concocted: he put her on the wrong train while he slipped back to Black Hawk in his failed scheme to have his way with Ántonia.

SUMMARY & ANALYSIS

---

## ANALYSIS: BOOK II, CHAPTERS VIII–XV

Frances Harling, the no-nonsense businesswoman of the novel, perfectly describes the core of Jim's affliction. Criticizing Jim over his affections for the hired girls, Frances says, "The problem with you, Jim, is that you're romantic." Frances's objection to Jim's social persona lies both in his withdrawal from society and in the glorified sense of glamour that he bestows upon Ántonia, Lena, and the rest of their kind. Frances, who speaks for the more respectable realms of Black Hawk society, represents a class of people whom Jim despises. Jim contrasts the staid propriety of a house full of "hand-painted china that must not be used" with the carefree charms of the free spirits he deems "my country girls."

The dancing pavilion brings the difference between the sheltered American daughters and the immigrant working girls into relief. As Jim observes, the presence of the dance hall upsets the established social order. With little to lose, the displaced immigrant girls from Bohemia, Denmark, and Norway take advantage of their working-class freedom to gain a foothold among the young men of Black Hawk, while the more respectable girls of established families are left to hang back in the shadows.

From the distanced perspective of a man writing a memoir, Jim can look back on this curious social order and analyze it as the natural evolution of the American immigrant experience. The same girls who were initially held back by barriers of language and wealth applied the strength of character acquired through hardship in order to better their lot in life. As a result, the servant girls of Jim's youth become the property-owning mistresses of his adulthood.

That such radical changes are afoot is clear from the pressing march of time. Jim himself is very conscious of the fleetingness of existence, soliloquizing that "when boys and girls are growing up, life can't stand still, not even in the quietest of country towns; and they have to grow up, whether they will or no." Although Jim clearly understands the inevitability of growing up, we get the sense that his romantic side is loath to do so.

Jim grows to dislike the stillness of Black Hawk, however, shuffling aimlessly as he does in his senior year among the "malcontent" in their "flimsy shelters." But at the same time, he longs to recapture the innocence and purity of his childhood affection for the domestic and the mundane, as shown when he hangs a May basket for young Nina Harling, taking a "melancholy pleasure" in the action.

As Book II comes to an end, the feeling that the characters are moving out of childhood and into the world of adulthood is nearly complete. The story's increasing emphasis on sexuality—including Cutter's bizarre attempt to sleep with Ántonia—reflects this transition. Jim's reluctance to grow up manifests itself most strongly in his inability to reconcile his emotional and sexual urges. When he attempts to kiss Ántonia in the same way that he has kissed Lena, she curtly but politely rebuffs him; he does not protest, but is pleased by her modesty. Although he is "not half as fond" of Lena as he is of Ántonia, it is Lena that he dreams of passionately embracing, and though he wishes it were Ántonia in her stead, he is never able to dream about her in the same way.

Ántonia, too, harbors nostalgia for a purer, more childlike past. She arranges for Jim to meet her and her friends at the river, in a last attempt to re-create old times. While her tears are ostensibly shed in longing for a lost Bohemia, she perhaps feels another grief—equally strong but subconscious—for the loss of her and Jim's shared childhood in the Nebraska countryside.

Once again, Cather reverts to the majesty of the landscape to provide a visual analogue for the nostalgia and sense of loss that her characters feel. As Jim and the girls continue to reminisce late into the afternoon, a plow emerges against the red disk of the setting sun, heroic in its loneliness, a symbol for the romantic imagination. But, inevitably, like the romantic imagination itself, this heroic image can enjoy only a fleeting moment of distorted importance. As the sun slowly sinks, the plow is returned "back to its own littleness" beneath the darkening sky, symbolizing how helpless humankind is in the face of indomitable forces of the universe such as time.

## BOOK III, CHAPTERS I–IV

### SUMMARY: CHAPTER I
At the university, Jim comes under the influence of a young scholar named Gaston Cleric. He takes rooms with an elderly couple on the edge of Lincoln and quickly becomes engrossed in his studies. During the summer, he remains in Lincoln to study Greek under the terms of his enrollment.

### SUMMARY: CHAPTER II
One evening, during the spring of his sophomore year, Jim is deep in thought when someone knocks at his door. He is slow to recognize his visitor, but soon realizes that it is Lena Lingard, dressed in her city finery. She explains to him that she has set up in Lincoln as a dressmaker, and she describes the details of her business affairs. When Jim asks after Ántonia, Lena explains that Ántonia has taken up work with Mrs. Gardener at the hotel and is engaged to Larry

Donovan. Jim greets this news with a mixture of pleasure and dismay, and he mentions an urge to go home and take care of her. Lena changes the subject to the theater, and Jim asks if she would like to get together for a theater outing in the near future. Lena agrees to this proposal and departs as quickly as she has come, leaving Jim among his books in the solitude of his study.

## SUMMARY: CHAPTER III
Throughout the spring, Jim and Lena attend a series of plays together. One play in particular, *Camille*, the story of a man's love for a woman dying of tuberculosis, affects them both very strongly.

## SUMMARY: CHAPTER IV
In addition to spending time with Lena at the theater, Jim visits her regularly at her dressmaking shop and takes Sunday breakfasts with her at her apartment. As the weeks wear on, Jim becomes less interested in his classes and spends more and more time hanging about with Lena and her circle. Near the end of the academic term, Cleric informs Jim that he has accepted an instructorship at Harvard College and wants Jim to accompany him east. After receiving the blessing of his grandfather, Jim resolves to leave Lincoln, and he visits Lena to tell her his decision. While sad to hear the news, she makes no attempt to hold him back. When the term ends, Jim returns home to be with his grandparents for a few weeks. He then makes a visit to his relatives in Virginia before joining Cleric in Boston.

---

## ANALYSIS: BOOK III, CHAPTERS I–IV
Book III reflects another major narrative shift in the novel: Jim's transition to college. Although Jim's move from the farm to Black Hawk—the break separating Books I and II—makes for a change of scenery, his sense of place is still firmly rooted in the nearby countryside that he roamed as a boy. But with his entry into the university at Lincoln in Book III, a more permanent rift between his past and his present begins to establish itself. Jim's initial impulse is to reject the lure of "impersonal" scholarship in favor of his "own naked land and the figures scattered upon it." He finds himself torn between study and memory, excited by the lure of learning new forms, but at the same time plunged back into thoughts of his past. In the face of the new, Jim finds the old people and ways "strengthened and simplified," though it is unclear whether such an improvement is more

a virtue of the past itself or a result of thinking about the past in a new way.

In either event, the nostalgia that Jim begins to feel at the university is extremely intense, and it begins to hamper his ability to live in the present. The people that he carries with him in his mind are so alive to him that he "scarcely stopped to wonder whether they were alive anywhere else, or how." Ántonia soon comes to display a similar tendency to live in the past at the expense of her present.

The idea that takes hold of Jim most strongly in the course of his study is the concept of *patria,* or loyalty to one's specific place of origin, a concept prominent in the works of the renowned Latin poet Virgil. The heart of *My Ántonia* lies not in its existence as an American novel, or even as a novel of the American Midwest, but rather as a fictionalized document of childhood in a town like Cather's own Red Cloud, Nebraska. The devotion that Cather, and by extension Jim, feels is not for the cosmopolitan present in which they are immersed but rather for the provincial countryside of their youth, which they carry in their hearts always.

Jim's complete separation of his Lincoln world from his Black Hawk world is undermined by the visit he receives from Lena Lingard. She acts as a link between his past and his present and continues to stand in Ántonia's place as an object of his desire. Jim's relationship with Lena is curiously sterile; although he spends a great deal of time with her, their interaction is rarely charged with the same quality of emotional intensity as his earlier interactions with Ántonia are.

With the security of his childhood and his early family life slipping away from him, Jim finds himself in an aimless and unhappy state. Cather makes use of a play (*Camille*) within the novel to illustrate Jim's mood, presenting his wistful perspective in the middle of a particularly wrenching theatergoing experience. As he watches the tragic story told in *Camille* unfold, Jim feels "helpless to prevent the closing of that chapter of idyllic love" in which the protagonist's "ineffable happiness was only to be the measure of his fall." The unhappy fate of the drama's male character is Jim's fate as well, and Cather suggests that art itself is of value as a reflection of our own emotions and experiences.

Jim marvels at the power of art to get at such universal truths "across long years and several languages," but at the same time he reveals his own subjective bias about art's meaning, asserting that "whenever and wherever that piece is put on, it is April." The play has crystallized for him a certain emotion that he associates with April, but in linking the play automatically to this emotion, he potentially limits the breadth of his actual experience.

## BOOK IV, CHAPTERS I–IV

### SUMMARY: CHAPTER I
Jim completes his academic program at Harvard in two years and returns to Black Hawk for summer vacation before entering law school. On the evening of his arrival, he is greeted at home by the Harlings. After Jim catches up with his family and friends, Frances brings up the subject of Ántonia. He knows that Larry Donovan never married Ántonia and that he left her with a child. Jim thinks bitterly of Ántonia's lot, lamenting her misfortunes.

### SUMMARY: CHAPTER II
On a trip to the town photographer to arrange a portrait of his grandparents, Jim notices a prominently placed picture of a baby on the wall. The photographer informs Jim that it is a likeness of Ántonia's baby, and that Ambrosch will be coming in to the studio to collect it over the weekend. On his way home from the photographer's, Jim stops at Mrs. Harling's and mentions to her his wish to learn more about Ántonia's plight. She suggests that he go to visit Widow Steavens, the tenant on the Burdens' old farmland.

### SUMMARY: CHAPTER III
At the beginning of August, Jim takes a horse and cart out to the countryside to visit Widow Steavens. She welcomes him warmly and invites him to stay the night, promising to speak to him of Ántonia after supper. That evening, Jim and the widow repair to the old sitting room upstairs, and she begins her story.

In the weeks leading up to her wedding, Ántonia had been hard at work, sewing various things for her new household and anxiously awaiting the approaching date. When Donovan had written to her soon after to inform her that his route as a train conductor had changed and that they would have to live in Denver, Ántonia was initially discouraged, but she quickly placed her doubts behind her. When the time to depart came, Ambrosch helped Ántonia pack up and drove her into Black Hawk to board the night train for Denver.

After receiving a couple of initial communications from Denver confirming Ántonia's safe arrival, the Shimerdas heard nothing from her for several weeks. Then, suddenly, she reappeared at home one day, unmarried and devastated by Donovan's desertion of her and subsequent running off to Mexico. Throughout the spring and summer, Ántonia worked in the fields, shutting herself in among her family. In the winter, she bore a child, to the surprise of her family, who had not observed her pregnancy because of the loose and bulky clothing that she had taken to wearing.

Widow Steavens concludes her story by telling Jim that Ántonia's baby is nearly two years old now, healthy and strong. Jim retires for the evening into the room he slept in as a boy, and he lays awake watching the moonlight and the windmill.

## SUMMARY: CHAPTER IV

The next afternoon, Jim walks over to the Shimerdas'. After Yulka shows him Ántonia's baby, he walks out to the fields to speak to Ántonia. They meet, clasp hands, and walk together to the site of Mr. Shimerda's grave. Jim tells her his plans for law school and of his life in the East. Ántonia tells him of her resolution to bring her daughter up into the world. As they walk across the fields together at sunset, Jim feels a strong nostalgia for the Nebraska landscape. At the edge of the field, Ántonia and Jim part ways. Jim gives his promise to return, and Ántonia gives her promise to remember him always. As Jim walks back to his old farmhouse alone at dark, he has the sense of two young children running along beside him.

## ANALYSIS: BOOK IV, CHAPTERS I–IV

With Jim at Harvard, away from the constancy of his Nebraska childhood, the narrative becomes even more piecemeal, and Jim's memory begins to skip around from story to story. Jim contrasts Ántonia's lot as a mother on the Nebraska prairie with that of her girlhood friends, Lena Lingard and Tiny Soderball, who in time come to establish themselves as women of fortune and position in San Francisco. The upward mobility that Lena and Tiny enjoy is somewhat undermined by Jim's lukewarm description of it: he remarks of Lena that she "had got on in the world" and of Tiny that "she was satisfied with her success, but not elated." For all of their victories, Lena and Tiny's lack of earnestness and enthusiasm does much to tarnish their achievements in Jim's eyes.

In contrast to these successful women in urban America stands Ántonia, who has returned to the country after a thwarted attempt to make a new life for herself in the big city. Like Jim, Ántonia has a powerful sense of place that supersedes all other considerations. But, unlike Jim, without the prospect of a career in front of her, she is quickly sucked back into her natural, if not native, environment.

Saddled with a child, deserted on the brink of marriage, Ántonia retreats to the idylls of her past in the face of an unacceptable present. Her labor is slow and intermittent, for, as she says to the Widow Steavens, "[I]f I start to work, I look around and forget to go on. It seems such a little while ago when Jim Burden and I was playing all over this country." To the romantic individual, a specific place becomes invested with the quality of an emotion felt at a specific time, and such a mind is slow to disassociate such remembrances in a changing situation. Ántonia prefers to live in the past and is fully aware of her denial of the reality of the present; despite the fact that her father is long since dead, for instance, Ántonia tells Jim that her father "is more real to me than almost anybody else."

What brings both Ántonia and Jim to an acceptance of change is their ability to come to terms with their own nostalgia. Rather than denying or feeling guilt about their yearnings to recapture and relive the old times, they indulge themselves by reminiscing. Thus, while their exteriors may shift radically, their interiors are constant and unchanging. This interior steadfastness gives them repose in the face of an unstable environment. Upon returning home for the summer before he enters law school, Jim sees the world changing, but he doesn't mind because what is truly important to him—the memories—remain the same.

## BOOK V, CHAPTERS I–III

*It was no wonder that her sons stood tall and*
*straight. She was a rich mine of life, like the founders*
*of early races.* (See QUOTATIONS, p. 53)

SUMMARY: CHAPTER I
Some twenty years later, Jim returns to Nebraska on his way home to New York from a business trip out west. His intention is to see Ántonia, of whom he has heard almost nothing in the intervening period except that she has married a fellow Bohemian named Cuzak and is raising a large family.

When his buggy arrives at the Cuzak farm, Jim is led up to the house by two young boys and welcomed into the kitchen by two older girls. As he prepares to sit down, Ántonia enters the room, but she fails to recognize him initially. Once she does, she is thrown into a rush of emotion and calls out to gather her children around her. Introductions are made, and Ántonia and Jim sit down in the kitchen to discuss old times and new times.

During their conversation, one of Ántonia's boys comes into the house to mourn the death of his dog. Ántonia consoles him, and the Cuzaks take Jim on a tour of their new fruit cave. Afterward, Jim is taken through the farmhouse and then on to the orchard. Another long talk of times gone by ensues, and Ántonia invites Jim to stay the night with them. Jim expresses his wish to sleep in the haymow with her sons, and Ántonia goes off to prepare supper while Jim heads out to milk cows with the boys.

At supper the group crowds into the kitchen, and afterward everyone settles in the parlor for some musical entertainment by the Cuzak children. After the concert, Ántonia brings out a box of photographs, and the children gather around as their mother leads Jim through the pictures. Ántonia tells stories until eleven, when Jim and the boys retire to the barn. The boys' giggles quickly give way to slumber, but Jim lays awake late into the night, thinking of Ántonia.

### SUMMARY: CHAPTER II

The next morning, Jim dresses in the barn and washes up by the windmill, entering the kitchen to find breakfast ready. In the afternoon, Cuzak returns with his oldest son and introduces him to Jim. Cuzak begins to describe the details of their trip into town, including a dance at which they encountered many of Ántonia's Bohemian acquaintances. Back at the house, as Ántonia serves a supper of geese and apples, the talk turns to Black Hawk, and the story of the violent murder-suicide involving Wick Cutter and his wife.

After the meal, Cuzak and Jim take a walk into the orchard, and Cuzak recounts for Jim the details of his early life. Confessing a loneliness for his old haunts in Bohemia and Vienna, Cuzak explains that the warmth of Ántonia's love and the energy of his large family has kept him free from despair.

## Summary: Chapter iii

The following day, after dinner, Jim leaves the Cuzaks. The whole family gathers to see him off as he departs, and Jim pulls away in the buggy as Ántonia waves her apron in farewell by the windmill.

In Black Hawk the next day, Jim is disappointed by the unfamiliar town, and is hard-pressed to occupy himself until the night express train arrives. Toward evening, Jim walks out beyond the outskirts of town and finds himself at home again. In his wanderings, he comes upon the first bit of the old road that leads out to the country farms. Although the track has largely been plowed under, Jim easily recognizes the way. He sits down by the overgrowth and watches the haystacks glowing in the sunlight.

---

## Analysis: Book v, Chapters i–iii

With twenty years gone by since their last encounter, it is no surprise that Ántonia fails to recognize Jim immediately when he arrives at her farm. Because of the interval in their acquaintance, it also follows that Jim's description of Ántonia should be an odd mixture of the familiar and the strange. He refers to her in one breath as "this woman" and in the next insists that her eyes could be none other than her own.

As the two warm up to each other, the awkwardness of lost time fades into the background, and Ántonia and Jim begin to enjoy each other's company in their old easy way. As Jim remembers, with the face-to-face encounter "the changes grew less apparent to me, her identity stronger." Still, Ántonia does not expect to find Jim childless, and this fact throws him into stark contrast with Ántonia, a mother to a large family. The difference in their domestic status owes perhaps to the difference in their environments: Jim, as an urban white-collar worker, has less need to rear children than the poor, farm-bound Cuzaks, who need all the labor they can get.

Ántonia is as invested in her relationship with the landscape as ever, as demonstrated by her carefully cultivated orchard. She endows the trees around her with human qualities, declaring much as Jim does earlier in his childhood that she loves them "as if they were people" and explaining that as she cared for them in their first growth "they were on my mind like children." Jim quickly reintegrates himself into such a landscape-oriented life in the countryside, and feels as he milks the cows with Ántonia's sons that "everything was as it should be."

In bringing out a box of photographs to display, Ántonia returns to a tangible resource that provokes a flood of memories. By educating her children in the tales of her past, she has made her past a part of her present, and the photographs help the memory of those old stories to live on. Memory lives largely on the strength of images, photographic or otherwise, and in recalling his feelings for Ántonia, Jim runs through a series of pictures from the past in his own head. At the same time, he finds that Ántonia "still had that something which fires the imagination," and is every bit as moved by the images of his return visit as he has been all these years by the pictures from his childhood.

Ultimately, more than the photographs or the mental images, it is the surrounding prairie landscape that comes to serve as an icon of the childhood idyll that Ántonia and Jim earlier share. After parting once again from Ántonia, Jim finds resolution and strength in a walk among the familiar, silent places of his youth, illustrating how the past still has a tremendous power to comfort him.

Although the road leading out to the old farms is largely grown over, it still serves as a useful landmark to those aware of its presence. Likewise, the map of memory is a key to the present for those who have lived through the past. In returning to his roots, Jim is taken by "what a little circle man's experience is" and resolves to renew his relationship with Ántonia and develop a bond with her family. Regardless of the missing years between them, Jim finds the key to a future with his childhood friend in the richness of what they hold in common—"the precious, the incommunicable past." Jim meditates on this shared past once again as the landscape closest to his heart lies quietly beneath the darkness that surrounds him.

# IMPORTANT QUOTATIONS EXPLAINED

1.    During that burning day when we were crossing Iowa, our talk kept returning to a central figure, a Bohemian girl whom we had both known long ago. More than any other person we remembered, this girl seemed to mean to us the country, the conditions, the whole adventure of our childhood.

This passage from the Introduction is the first the reader hears of Ántonia. The narrator of the Introduction, who grew up with Jim and Ántonia in Nebraska, describes a train ride taken with Jim many years later and details their conversation about Ántonia. They agreed that Ántonia, more than any other person, seemed to represent the world they had grown up in, to the point that speaking her name evokes "people and places" and "a quiet drama . . . in one's brain." This quotation is important because it establishes that Ántonia will both evoke and symbolize the vanished past of Jim's childhood in Nebraska. It situates Ántonia as the central character in Jim's story and explains Jim's preoccupation with her by connecting her to his memories of the past. Finally, it establishes Jim's character with its implication that Jim shares the unnamed narrator's romantic inclination to dwell on the past and to allow people and places to take on an extraordinarily emotional, nostalgic significance.

2.　　"I never know you was so brave, Jim," she went on
　　　　comfortingly. "You is just like big mans; you wait for
　　　　him lift his head and then you go for him. Ain't you
　　　　feel scared a bit? Now we take that snake home and
　　　　show everybody. Nobody ain't seen in this kawn-tree
　　　　so big snake like you kill."

Ántonia speaks these lines in Book I, Chapter VII, praising Jim for
having killed the rattlesnake. Jim is angry with Ántonia for failing to
warn him about the snake (in a moment of panic, she screams out in
her native language), and she quickly appeases him by gushing
about his bravery and manliness. The quote captures Ántonia's way
of speaking in the early part of the novel, as she is learning English;
it also represents a moment of transition in Jim's relationship with
her. Because she is older than Jim, Ántonia has had a tendency to
treat him somewhat condescendingly, to Jim's increasing frustra-
tion. After he proves his strength by killing the rattlesnake, she
regards him with a new respect and never talks down to him again.
She may never love Jim romantically, but at this moment, she clearly
comes to regard him as an equal and as someone very special to her.

3.     "Why aren't you always nice like this, Tony?"
       "How nice?"
       "Why, just like this; like yourself. Why do you all
the time try to be like Ambrosch?"
       She put her arms under her head and lay back,
looking up at the sky. "If I live here, like you, that is
different. Things will be easy for you. But they will be
hard for us."

This dialogue from Book I, Chapter XIX, occurs as Jim and Ántonia
sit on the roof of the chicken house, watching the electrical storm.
The two have grown apart somewhat following Mr. Shimerda's suicide, as Jim has begun to attend school and Ántonia has been forced
to spend her time working on the farm. Jim has found himself dis-
mayed by Ántonia's increasing coarseness and her pride in her own
strength. As they sit watching the lightning storm, Jim feels his old
intimacy returning, and he brings himself to ask Ántonia why she
has changed. Ántonia understands Jim's question and, because she
is four years older, understands better than he does why their lives
have begun to move in separate directions. Jim has opportunities
and a bright future ahead of him, but for Ántonia, life now means
simply helping her family get by. Ántonia acknowledges this unal-
terable circumstance with her customarily wise simplicity: "Things
will be easy for you. But they will be hard for us."

QUOTATIONS

4.    Presently we saw a curious thing: There were no
      clouds, the sun was going down in a limpid, gold-
      washed sky. Just as the lower edge of the red disc
      rested on the high fields against the horizon, a great
      black figure suddenly appeared on the face of the sun.
      We sprang to our feet, straining our eyes toward it. In
      a moment we realized what it was. On some upland
      farm, a plough had been left standing in the field. The
      sun was sinking just behind it. Magnified across the
      distance by the horizontal light, it stood out against
      the sun, was exactly contained within the circle of the
      disk; the handles, the tongue, the share—black against
      the molten red. There it was, heroic in size, a picture
      writing on the sun.
          Even while we whispered about it, our vision
      disappeared; the ball dropped and dropped until the
      red tip went beneath the earth. The fields below us
      were dark, the sky was growing pale, and that
      forgotten plough had sunk back to its own littleness
      somewhere on the prairie.

This passage from Book II, Chapter XIV, recounts a sunset that Jim and Ántonia watch the summer after Jim graduates from high school. Gradually, the sun sinks behind a plow on the horizon, so the plow is superimposed on the red sun, "black against molten red." The passage is an excellent example of Cather's famous ability to evoke the landscape, creating a sensuous and poetic picture of a sunset on the Nebraska prairie. It also indicates the extraordinary psychological connection that Cather's characters feel with their landscape, as the setting sun perfectly captures the quiet, somewhat bittersweet moment the characters are experiencing—they care for one another and have had a wonderful day together, but they are growing up and will soon go their separate ways.

The image of the plow superimposed on the sun also suggests a symbolic connection between human culture (the plow) and the nature (the sun). As the plow fills up the disk of the sun, the two coexist in perfect harmony, just as Jim recalls the idyllic connection between the natural landscape and the settlements in Nebraska. But as the sun sinks beneath the horizon, the plow dwindles to insignificance ("its own littleness"), suggesting that, in the relationship between humankind and environment, environment is dominant.

5.     She lent herself to immemorial human attitudes which
we recognize by instinct as universal and true. I had
not been mistaken. She was a battered woman now,
not a lovely girl; but she still had that something
which fires the imagination, could still stop one's
breath for a moment by a look or gesture that
somehow revealed the meaning in common things.
She had only to stand in the orchard, to put her hand
on a little crab tree and look up at the apples, to make
you feel the goodness of planting and tending and
harvesting at last. All the strong things of her heart
came out in her body, that had been so tireless in
serving generous emotions.
     It was no wonder that her sons stood tall and
straight. She was a rich mine of life, like the founders
of early races.

This quotation, which concludes Book v, Chapter i, finds the adult
Jim still contemplating the fascination he feels for Ántonia. Here
he attributes her significance to her nurturing and generous presence, which suggests an enviable fullness of life. Ántonia evokes
"immemorial human attitudes which we recognize by instinct as
universal and true" because she is full of love and loyalty. As Jim
portrays it, Ántonia is a "rich mine of life," an inexhaustible
source of love and will from which others draw strength and
warmth. This portrayal explains why Ántonia lingers so prominently in the minds of so many people from Jim's childhood (Jim,
Lena, the narrator of the introduction). In her presence they have
been filled with the love and strength that she exudes, and they will
never forget the way it made them feel.

     Apart from standing as the novel's final important analysis of
Ántonia, this quote is important because it reveals the psychological
changes that the passage of time has wrought in Jim. Whereas
before he avoided Ántonia for twenty years because he did not want
to see the lovely girl he knew transformed into a hardened, over-
worked matron, he can now see beyond Ántonia's age to her essen-
tial inner quality, which he finds can still "stop one's breath." This
newfound connection to the present indicates that Jim can finally
move beyond his dreamlike preoccupation with his nostalgia for his
youth and contemplate Ántonia as more than a symbol of the past.

# KEY FACTS

FULL TITLE
*My Ántonia*

AUTHOR
Willa Cather

TYPE OF WORK
Novel

GENRE
Frontier fiction, autobiographical fiction

LANGUAGE
English

TIME AND PLACE WRITTEN
1917, New Hampshire

DATE OF FIRST PUBLICATION
1918

NARRATOR
The main part of the story is Jim Burden's memoir narrated in his first-person voice, from the perspective of an older man looking back on his childhood. The introduction to the novel is narrated by an unnamed individual, one of Jim's childhood acquaintances. Like Jim, this narrator uses a friendly, first-person voice.

POINT OF VIEW
Except for the introduction, written from the perspective of the unnamed narrator, the entire novel is written from Jim's perspective.

TONE
Jim's attitude toward his story is somewhat sad, extremely nostalgic, and full of yearning for a lost past. Throughout Book v, as he narrates the story of his reunion with Ántonia, he becomes much more optimistic and less elegiac in mood.

TENSE
Past

SETTING (TIME)
  1880s–1910s

SETTING (PLACE)
  In and around Black Hawk, Nebraska; also Lincoln, Nebraska

PROTAGONIST
  Jim Burden

MAJOR CONFLICT
  Jim has an extremely close, loving relationship with his childhood friend Ántonia, but their friendship is tested by the different paths their lives take them down, as Jim acquires an education while Ántonia is forced to work to help support her family. As a secondary conflict, Jim, a middle-aged lawyer, looks back longingly toward his childhood with Ántonia but feels he has lost it forever; his feelings of nostalgia impede him from reestablishing contact with the real Ántonia, now the matriarch of a large family in Nebraska. On a more concrete level, Ántonia must struggle against various hardships, such as the death of her father and her fiancé's betrayal of her.

RISING ACTION
  Many modernist authors broke from dramatic or narrative conventions; *My Ántonia* does so by avoiding a conventional plot shape with rising action, climax, and falling action. Still, as Ántonia's life becomes fraught with increasing hardship, we might say that her father's suicide, the betrayal of her fiancé, and the birth of her child act as rising action. In Jim's life, his move to Black Hawk, his time with Lena, and the dances all serve as rising action in his transition from childhood to adulthood.

CLIMAX
  The structure of *My Ántonia* does not yield one singular moment of dramatic intensity in which the conflict is resolved. The novel becomes calmer and less conflicted as the final books progress, leading to a warmly optimistic conclusion that is not the result of any definitive struggle. The closest thing the novel has to a climactic moment is Jim's reunion with Ántonia, twenty years after their last meeting.

FALLING ACTION
If Jim's reunion with Ántonia is taken as the climax, then the falling action is his time at the Cuzak farm as he grows to know and admire Ántonia's husband and children, and resolves to spend more time with them.

THEMES
Humankind's relationship to the past; humankind's relationship to environment; the immigrant experience in America; the traditional nature of late nineteenth-century American frontier values

MOTIFS
Religion, childhood, and adulthood

SYMBOLS
The Nebraska landscape, the plow

FORESHADOWING
The information divulged in the Introduction contains the blueprint for everything to come in the novel; in a sense, the whole novel is foreshadowed. Also, Ántonia's statement to Jim that things will be easy for him but hard for her foreshadows his eventual departure for college and a high-powered job and her difficult life on the prairie.

# Study Questions & Essay Topics

## Study Questions

1.  *Who is the protagonist of* My Ántonia, *Ántonia or Jim?*

While many have argued that Ántonia is the protagonist of the
novel, she always remains at arm's length from the reader, accessi-
ble only through Jim's imagination and memory of her. When Jim
scribbles a title onto his manuscript, he initially writes "Ántonia,"
but then revises it to "My Ántonia." Thus, the Ántonia we see is
Jim's Ántonia, and while she is a driving force behind Jim's recollection, Jim's mind and feelings are still at the center of the narrative,
and his actions still determine the shape of the novel. When Jim
moves first to Lincoln and then to Cambridge and New York, Ántonia recedes as an important character, even if she dominates Jim's
thoughts when he is around her. *My Ántonia* is most properly considered a novel of Jim's education.

2.    *What is the nature of Jim's affection for Ántonia? Does*
      *Ántonia reciprocate these feelings, or is the quality of her*
      *affection somehow different? Is it fair to call their*
      *relationship a love relationship?*

Jim has a romanticized affection for Ántonia but not quite a romantic affection. He is unable to imagine her in the same light as Lena
Lingard, for whom he feels a coarser but perhaps more practical
passion. Still, the idealized love that Jim feels for Ántonia eclipses
the strength of Ántonia's feeling for him. Because she is somewhat
older, and because her plight as an immigrant's daughter creates
many hardships, she has less time and energy to devote to romantic
imaginations of Jim: while Jim is thinking about his feelings for
Ántonia, Ántonia is busy trying to help her family survive after the
death of her father.

      Additionally, as young man born and raised in America, Jim
belongs to the dominant culture and is perhaps more easily able to
disregard Ántonia's cultural differences than Ántonia herself is.
Having immigrated to America as a teenager, Ántonia is naturally
more aware of her own differences from Jim, simply because to her
the environment in which she lives never seems quite like her native
environment; as a result, she is slightly more insular about her affections than Jim, with the result that her feelings become somewhat
inscrutable as the novel progresses. This side of Ántonia seems most
strongly demonstrated by her eventual decision to marry Cuzak, a
Bohemian immigrant like herself. Nevertheless, she is clearly of a
romantic persuasion, and the love she holds for Jim is akin to what
an older sister might feel for a younger brother. Thus, the love that
comes to develop between Ántonia and Jim falls somewhere in
between familial and romantic affection.

3.   *Where does Jim fall within the social structure of Black
     Hawk that he outlines?*

Jim describes a social structure in Black Hawk that divides the
respectable establishment from the generally less-respected immigrants. While Jim is by default a member of the respectable establishment, his relatively recent arrival in Black Hawk and his
vociferous rejection of established values serve to place him outside
of its bounds. Jim's class and upbringing ensure that he will never be
an outcast on the level of the immigrant girls, but his affection for
them and his affiliation with them puts him in a unique and ambiguous position within the Black Hawk social hierarchy.

4.     *Why does Jim choose to live in New York City if he truly feels most at home in Nebraska?*

Jim paints a very sentimental and idealized picture of Nebraska, but this picture is a memory of a time that has long since passed. While Jim could potentially return to Black Hawk to practice law, his high-powered New York City job is a logical extension of his high-powered education. When he returns to Nebraska to visit Ántonia, he is greatly moved by the beauty and simplicity of her rural life, but he finds Black Hawk nearly intolerable and is at a loss for things to do there. Jim's proper sphere as an adult is certainly not Nebraska, although his fond memories of childhood will always remain there, and his resolution to make more periodic returns to his childhood home is certainly a positive move on his part. The peculiarities of Jim's life are such that, just as he does not quite fit into the rigid social hierarchy of Black Hawk as a young man, he does not quite fit into any geographical environment as an adult. He seems to be fated to live in one place while always thinking fondly of another.

# SUGGESTED ESSAY TOPICS

1. What is the role of the landscape in the novel? How does the novel thematize the relationship between man and environment?

2. What is Ántonia's relationship to her native Bohemia? Does she have stronger feelings for Bohemia or for Nebraska? What does Ántonia's predicament say about the lives of immigrants during the time of the novel?

3. How does the structure of the novel serve to emphasize some of its overriding themes?

4. Can Jim's view of Ántonia be considered reductive or patronizing in any way? Consider that Cather is a woman writing from the perspective of a man writing about a woman.

# REVIEW & RESOURCES

## QUIZ

1.  What town is near the Burdens' farm?

    A.  Black Hawk, Nebraska
    B.  Red Wing, Michigan
    C.  Black Hawk, Illinois
    D.  Red Wing, Kansas

2.  How does Ántonia's father die?

    A.  He has a heart attack
    B.  He is gored by a bull
    C.  He commits suicide
    D.  He is lost in a snowstorm

3.  With whom does Jim live for most of the novel?

    A.  His parents
    B.  His grandparents
    C.  His aunt's family
    D.  His foster parents

4.  What nationality are the Shimerdas?

    A.  German
    B.  Czechoslovakian
    C.  Romanian
    D.  Bohemian

5.  What does Otto decide to do when the Burdens move into town?

    A.  Travel west
    B.  Buy the farm
    C.  Marry Ántonia
    D.  Move with them

6.  Where does Jim attend college?

    A.  The University of Chicago
    B.  Oberlin
    C.  The University of Michigan and Princeton
    D.  The University of Nebraska and Harvard

7.  When does the blizzard occur?

    A.  Christmas
    B.  Jim's fifth birthday
    C.  Ántonia's twelfth birthday
    D.  Jim's eleventh birthday

8.  Which character moves to San Fransisco?

    A.  Lena
    B.  Ántonia
    C.  Jim
    D.  Ambrosch

9.  To whom does Ántonia first become engaged?

    A.  Cuzak
    B.  Jim
    C.  Larry Donovan
    D.  Samson d'Arnault

10. Where does Ántonia work after leaving the Harlings?

    A.  At the Shimerda farm
    B.  At Wick Cutter's
    C.  At the dancing pavilion
    D.  At a dressmaker's shop

11. To whom does Jim dedicate his commencement oration?

    A.  His grandfather
    B.  His grandmother
    C.  Ántonia
    D.  Ántonia's father

12. Who subdues the snake?

    A. Jim
    B. Ántonia
    C. Mr. Burden
    D. Otto

13. How does Pavel injure himself?

    A. He cuts his hand on a plowshare
    B. He nearly drowns in the creek
    C. He falls
    D. He sprains his wrist

14. What does Lena do in Black Hawk?

    A. She is a housekeeper
    B. She is a dressmaker
    C. She is a dancing instructor
    D. She is a housewife

15. Who plays the piano at the Boys' Home dance?

    A. Jim
    B. Ántonia
    C. Mrs. Harling
    D. Samson d'Arnault

16. Who begins the dancing in Black Hawk?

    A. The Harlings
    B. The Vannis
    C. Ántonia
    D. The Burdens

17. With which of the following men does Jim fight?

    A. Mr. Harling
    B. Gaston Cleric
    C. Wick Cutter
    D. Mr. Shimerda

REVIEW & RESOURCES

18. Who becomes Jim's tutor in Lincoln?

    A.  Gaston Cleric
    B.  Lena
    C.  Ambrosch
    D.  Yulka

19. What play do Jim and Lena see together?

    A.  *The Merchant of Venice*
    B.  *Candide*
    C.  *O Pioneers!*
    D.  *Camille*

20. When was My Ántonia orginally published?

    A.  1864
    B.  1873
    C.  1905
    D.  1918

21. Where did Willa Cather live before moving to Nebraska?

    A.  California
    B.  Virginia
    C.  Washington, D.C.
    D.  Bohemia

22. What is Jim's profession when he writes the memoir?

    A.  Cook
    B.  Farmer
    C.  Lawyer
    D.  Senator

23. How many years pass between the last two books of the novel?

    A.  20
    B.  10
    C.  5
    D.  2_

24. Who abandons Ántonia before their wedding?

    A. Cuzak
    B. Jim
    C. Micky
    D. Donovan

25. From whom does Jim seek information about Ántonia when he visits Black Hawk before starting law school?

    A. Mrs. Cutter
    B. Widow Steavens
    C. Nina Harling
    D. Ambrosch

# SUGGESTIONS FOR FURTHER READING

BLOOM, HAROLD, ed. *Willa Cather's* MY ÁNTONIA: *Modern Critical Interpretations.* New York: Chelsea House, 1988.

CATHER, WILLA. *O Pioneers! and Other Tales of the Prairie.* New York: Doubleday, 1999.

DAICHES, DAVID. *Willa Cather: A Critical Introduction.* Ithaca, New York: Cornell University Press, 1951.

GERBER, PHILIP. *Willa Cather.* Boston: Twayne Publishers, 1975.

LEE, HERMIONE. *Willa Cather: Double Lives.* New York: Pantheon, 1989.

O'BRIEN, SHARON, ed. *New Essays on My Ántonia.* New York: Cambridge University Press, 1999.

SMITH, HENRY NASH. Virgin Land: *The American West as Symbol and Myth.* Cambridge: Harvard University Press, 1971.

TURNER, FREDERICK JACKSON. *The Frontier in American History.* New York: Dover, 1996.

REVIEW & RESOURCES

## A Note on the Type

The typeface used in SparkNotes study guides is Sabon, created by master typographer Jan Tschichold in 1964. Tschichold revolutionized the field of graphic design twice: first with his use of asymmetrical layouts and sanserif type in the 1930s when he was affiliated with the Bauhaus, then by abandoning assymetry and calling for a return to the classic ideals of design. Sabon, his only extant typeface, is emblematic of his latter program: Tschichold's design is a recreation of the types made by Claude Garamond, the great French typographer of the Renaissance, and his contemporary Robert Granjon. Fittingly, it is named for Garamond's apprentice, Jacques Sabon.

# SPARKNOTES
# TEST PREPARATION
# GUIDES

The SparkNotes team figured it was time to cut standardized tests down to size. We've studied the tests for you, so that SparkNotes test prep guides are:

## *Smarter:*
Packed with critical-thinking skills and test-
taking strategies that will improve your score.

## *Better:*
Fully up to date, covering all new features of the tests,
with study tips on every type of question.

## *Faster:*
Our books cover exactly what you need to
know for the test. No more, no less.

# SparkNotes Study Guides: